Baptism in the Holy Spirit

Max Turner

Professor of New Testament Studies
London Bible College

GROVE BOOKS LIMITED
RIDLEY HALL RD CAMBRIDGE CB3 9HU

Contents

First Impression October 2000
ISSN 1470-8531
ISBN 1 85174 447 9

1

Introduction: Crucial Questions About Baptism in/with the Holy Spirit

People picking up this book are liable already to have considerable vested interests in the topic. And whether they belong to the Pentecostal tradition (and its spiritual heirs), to more traditional Evangelical circles, or to those with a more sacramental spirituality, most will be acutely aware that issues of 'baptism in/with Holy Spirit' (henceforth 'bhs') are hotly contended ones.

We can usefully distinguish two poles round which the questions cluster: the pole of biblical exegesis; and the pole of today's church, with its theology and experience. At the biblical pole we have questions such as:

- What did John the Baptist mean by the promise that the coming messiah would baptize with Holy Spirit (and fire)?
- How did Luke understand this, and what relevance did he think it would have for disciples of his own generation and those to follow?
- How does his understanding relate to the teaching of John and Paul?

At the pole of today's church we may be more interested in questions like:

- How do we best understand and evaluate the various experiences of Spirit-baptism in recent church history?
- Is an experience of Spirit-baptism essential for the practice of spiritual gifts?
- How should we promote and sustain a vibrant charismatic and missionary spirituality?

Of course, I am not suggesting the two poles, and the questions that cluster around them, are unrelated! Indeed the very complexity of the topic is partly the result of the many different ways the questions at the two poles have been related.

This booklet will begin by outlining something of the variety of modern understandings of bhs (chapter 2). I will then, in chapter 3, describe and assess the dominant twentieth-century interpretation of bhs, that of classical Pentecostalism and its developments. In chapter 4 I shall look at criticisms of, and proposed modifications to, this view. In the final chapter I will move towards more theological and pastoral conclusions, addressing the questions at the contemporary church pole. Of course, in a booklet like this I will not be able to give detailed argument. For that you will need to look elsewhere.[1]

---

1 Such as to Max Turner, *The Holy Spirit and Spiritual Gifts: Then and Now* (Carlisle: Paternoster, 1999).

2

'Baptism in/with Holy Spirit'
in the Modern Church

Intense interest in the nature and significance of bhs goes back far. We could probably even trace it to the writings of one of Wesley's contemporaries, John Fletcher, vicar of Madeley, in the 1770s. Others would point to the Irvingite movement of the 1830s. Certainly from 1850 onwards bhs was a widespread subject of preaching, spiritual conventions, pamphlets, guides to the 'higher Christian life,' and other works. It was the Pentecostal movement(s), however, which carried interest in bhs throughout the world. They started as recently as 1906, but their numbers have now swelled to some 500 million—amounting to almost a third of the whole church. Not even the apostolic church grew that fast.

Emerging Different 'Second Blessing' Understandings of BHS

While bhs was a common preaching topic, we need to recognize that people meant rather different things by it. Even amongst those who thought bhs was some kind of 'second blessing' granted to mature believers, we find numerous variations.

John Wesley had argued that Christians should receive a crisis experience of 'Christian Perfection,' following which they would not commit known sin. Fletcher was the first to identify this with the Pentecostal event of Acts 2 (and also first to coin the phrase 'baptism with the Holy Spirit' to refer to it, a phrase not found in the NT). In the predominantly Wesleyan Evangelicalism of North America people searched for—and of many it was claimed they attained—this experience of 'entire sanctification' or 'higher life' or 'holiness' through bhs.

From 1850 to 1899 there was a gradual shift towards using the term bhs more exclusively to mean 'empowering for service/mission,' rather than 'sanctification'—though, for many, 'sanctification' had included such empowering. In 1900 C F Parham set his students (in Topeka, Kansas) the task of discovering what was taken as the 'evidence' of the bhs in Acts. They concluded it was 'tongues.' They met to pray for a bhs with speaking in tongues, and from early 1901 the college began to experience this.[2] They understood their experience primarily as empowering for mission, Parham regarding 'tongues' as miraculous ability to address foreigners in languages unknown to the evangelist.

2   Church of God revival meetings were reporting outbreaks of tongues in the mid 1890s.

William Seymour (the leader of the Azusa Street revival in Los Angeles that began in 1906) came to oppose the view that 'tongues' was essentially intrinsic to bhs. Instead, he emphasized bhs as being flooded with the love of God and power for service. While the majority of the Pentecostal movements were to uphold tongues as the 'initial physical evidence,' others were willing to point to prophecy, praise, singing, dancing, and a variety of different responses, as evidence of bhs.

In Britain, in the 1960s, the same decade as the outbreak of the Charismatic Movement, Martin Lloyd-Jones was expounding bhs as an experience of sublime assurance, and of the sanctifying and empowering presence of God, more in continuity with Puritan and revivalist teaching. His sermon series on the subject was published after his death.[3]

The dominant understanding of mainline Pentecostals today is expressed in the words of David Petts, Principal of the Assemblies of God college, Mattersey Hall, since 1978:

When Pentecostals talk about the baptism in the Holy Spirit, they generally mean an experience of the Spirit's power accompanied by speaking in tongues as on the Day of Pentecost. The terminology is derived from Acts 1.5…The experience is usually closely associated with [many would say 'exclusively identified with'] enduement with power for service (Acts 1.8) and is understood to be 'subsequent to and distinct from regeneration.'[4]

Explanations of BHS as Beginning at Conversion.

We need also to remember that a very significant set of different groups—partly reacting to different types of second- or third-blessing claims—maintain that bhs should be understood primarily as the initial conversional, or regenerational, 'salvation' of the believer. This position is common ground to a surprisingly wide variety of views.

John Stott and F D Bruner, as traditional Evangelicals, have both expounded the position in an 'anti-charismatic' way.[5] For them bhs means being 'born again' of the Spirit (see John 3.3, 5)—essentially conversion—and it is not necessarily particularly experiential.

Theologians of the Charismatic Renewal Movement (especially those in the Roman Catholic sector) usually take the term bhs itself to refer to the gift

3   M Lloyd-Jones, *Joy Unspeakable: Power and Renewal in the Holy Spirit* (Eastbourne: Kingsway, 1984), M Eaton, *Baptism with the Spirit: The Teaching of Martin Lloyd-Jones* (Leicester: IVP, 1989).
4   D Petts, 'The Baptism in the Holy Spirit: The Theological Distinctive' in Keith Warrington (ed), *Pentecostal Perspectives* (Carlisle: Paternoster, 1998), pp 98–119.
5   J R W Stott, *The Baptism and Fullness of the Holy Spirit* (Leicester: IVP, 1975 [1964]), F D Bruner, *A Theology of the Holy Spirit: The Pentecostal Experience and the New Testament Witness* (Grand Rapids: Eerdmans, 1970).

of the Spirit given in the sacraments of baptism and confirmation. They prefer other terms, such as 'release of the Spirit,' 'renewal in the Spirit' or 'filling with the Spirit' for what Pentecostals mean by bhs.

Those in the 'Third Wave' movement, which was originally led by John Wimber, usually take bhs as providing the resources for all Christian life and charismata, but do not require that the initial 'moment' of bhs is itself necessarily 'charismatic.'

The influential writers James Dunn and David Pawson both interpret bhs as the initial reception of the Spirit, and expect it to be profoundly experiential.[6] Pawson (not Dunn) argues bhs would normally be accompanied by tongues.

Some other charismatic theologians (most notably Henry Lederle) take bhs not just as the single initial event of Spirit-reception, but as a way of speaking about the whole of Christian (essentially charismatic) life in the Spirit, from beginning to end.[7]

Where Does This All Leave Us and What is the Way Forward?

The above would certainly suggest that God graciously meets his people when they whole-heartedly seek him, and that he does so in a variety ways. But it does not suggest there is a single distinct identifiable 'experience,' which we might all agree to label 'bhs.' The reason for this is not merely because experiences are so varied, but also because we come with differing pre-understandings of what we mean by bhs. But it is the vast and energetic Pentecostal and Charismatic movements that have put bhs at the head of our agenda, and so it is to their interpretation that we turn in the next chapter.

---

6   J Dunn, *Baptism in the Holy Spirit* (London: SCM, 1970), D Pawson, *The Normal Christian Birth* (London: Hodder, 1989), *idem*, *Jesus Baptizes in One Holy Spirit* (London: Hodder, 1997).
7   H I Lederle, *Treasures Old and New: Interpretations of 'Spirit-Baptism' in the Charismatic Renewal Movement* (Peabody: Hendrickson, 1988).

3

Pentecostal Reading of the NT Concept of 'Baptism in Holy Spirit'

Pentecostals very much understand Luke-Acts as their story—it is Luke who gives unique prominence to Jesus baptizing with Holy Spirit (Lk 3.16 [= Mt 3.11, Mk 1.8, John 1.33]; Acts 1.5; 11.16). So we shall address their understanding of Luke-Acts first, then broaden the picture to John and Paul.

Pentecostal Interpretation of Luke-Acts

This usually highlights five cardinal points.

a. Jesus as the Model for Christians Jesus' experience at the Jordan (Lk 3.21-22) serves as a paradigm for all later believers—and it is clearly an empowering for service.

b. Pentecost as the Model for Christians The disciples' experience at Pentecost also provides a normal pattern for the church. They were already 'saved' believers, and they receive the Spirit as 'power from on high' to witness (Luke 24.49; Acts 1.8) as the fulfilment of John the Baptist's promise 'he will baptize you with Holy Spirit and fire' (Luke 3.17; Acts 1.5).

c. Peter's Speech Confirms the Pattern In Acts 2 Peter identifies the Spirit as Joel's promised 'Spirit of prophecy.' He then establishes that this gift is only given to those who are already God's repentant people ('Upon my servants...I will pour out my Spirit...and they will prophesy,' 2.18), and that the gift is promised to all who repent and are baptized (2.38-39).

d. The Rest of Acts Confirms the Paradigm Thus *the Samaritans* were clearly 'saved' and baptized believers (8.12, 16) some days before they received the Spirit (8.17). And their Spirit-baptism was sufficiently dramatic to make Simon Magus jealous for the power to confer it (8.18-19)! *Paul* becomes a believer on the Damascus Road, at least three days before he received healing and was filled with the Spirit for his missionary task (9.9, 15–17). The *Cornelius story* is told with multiple allusions to the Pentecost narrative (including the dramatic outburst of tongues 10.45-46), and from Peter's perspective the events are so similar that it reminds him of Jesus' words about John's promise (11.15-16). Cornelius' household have been baptized in Holy Spirit. The 'twelve' in *Ephesus* were clearly 'believers' (19.2— and Luke specifically calls them 'disciples,' 19.1) who had been baptized (though only with John's baptism). But Paul's question in 19.2 assumes the possibility of Christians without the Spirit, and their answer confirms it! They had not even heard of the gift. Accordingly Paul rebaptizes them, and then, subsequently, lays hands on them. As a consequence they receive the

7

Spirit with speaking in tongues and prophecy (19.5-6). Thus even if one were to claim that the twelve only really became Christians when Paul baptized them (19.5), their bhs comes after that event.

e. The Spirit in Luke is Exclusively Empowering for Service In Luke, reception of the Spirit is not about experiencing salvation, but always concerns empowering members of the saved community for witness. In this respect, two related descriptive terms applied to Spirit-reception are of great importance in Pentecostal teaching: (a) 'separability'—meaning that the actions of the Spirit in bhs are distinct from those involved in regeneration and entry into the life of salvation; and (b) 'subsequence'—meaning bhs follows logically, and normally temporally, the gift of regeneration.

On the above five cardinal points nearly all Pentecostal expositors have agreed, and the case has been strengthened and refined by Pentecostal NT scholars such as Stronstad, Penney, and especially Menzies.[8] Indeed virtually all specialists in Luke-Acts—even from outside the Pentecostal/Charismatic traditions—agree two points.[9] Firstly, for Luke the Spirit is largely the 'Spirit of prophecy,' in Acts especially as an 'empowering for mission.' And secondly, Luke shows relatively little interest in the Spirit as the power of the spiritual, ethical and religious renewal of the individual.

That agreement breaks down, however, within this vital second point. Some wish to affirm that 'relatively little interest' should be rewritten 'no interest whatever'—because they think Luke views the Spirit exclusively as prophetic empowering. Others disagree. We will need to tease out the issues in more detail in chapter 4.

Pentecostal Interpretation of John

The Fourth Gospel is seen to complement the above picture from Luke-Acts in an important way. For John, the disciples are already 'born from above' (3.3; or 'born of water and Spirit,' 3.5), within the ministry of Jesus—at the latest by 20.22. But at that point they have still to receive the Spirit-Paraclete promised in John 14-16. This second gift is to be sent by the ascended Lord from God's right hand (15.26, *cf* 14.16, 26). So it corresponds to Pentecost (and to the Baptist's promise of bhs in John 1.33). John thus offers all believers a two stage giving of the Spirit—first for salvation, then, later, as an empowering baptism with the Spirit-Paraclete.

Pentecostal Interpretation of Paul

Pentecostals recognize that for Paul the gift of the Spirit is essential for salvation. For Paul the believer 'begins' Christian existence by receiving the

<hr />

8   R P Menzies, *Empowered for Witness: The Spirit in Luke-Acts* (Sheffield: SAP, 1994).
9   For detail, see Turner, *Power from on High: The Spirit in Israel's Restoration and Witness in Luke-Acts* (Sheffield: SAP, 1996) chs 1–2; *idem*, *Spirit*, ch 2.

Spirit (Gal 3.3-5). Only by the Spirit are we initially 'washed, sanctified and justified' (1 Cor 6.11). The Spirit brings us the new covenant 'life' promised in Ezek 36-37 (1 Thess 4.7–8); it is only by the Spirit that we exchange the 'death' of existence 'according to the flesh' for new creation 'life' (Gal 5–6; Rom 7–8; 2 Cor 3–5) and sonship (Gal 4.4–6; Rom 8.14–16 and elsewhere). For Paul the very essence of this Christian life is profound, and continuing, Christ-centred encounter with God (Gal 2.19–20; Phil 1.21, 3.10). Salvation is 'union with Christ'—but this is only first made possible (and then maintained) through reception of the Spirit of God who now also comes to the Christian as the 'Spirit of Christ' (Rom 8.9–11; Gal 4.6; Phil 1.19). And Paul can affirm the corollary, 'anyone who does not have the Spirit of Christ, that person does not belong to him' (Rom 8.9b). From this, most Pentecostals normally recognize that from a Pauline perspective a Christian without the gift of the Spirit would be a contradiction in terms.

What of 'separability' and 'subsequence' in Paul? In addition to what we have just said, it is equally clear that Paul expects the gift of the Spirit to involve profoundly charismatic experiences (see, for example, Gal 3.3–5; 1 Thess 5.19–20; 1 Cor 12–14; Rom 12). And at the heart of the most detailed of these discussions, Pentecostals find the evidence for an element of 'separability' and 'subsequence' in Paul. 1 Cor 12.8–11 refers to a special coherent set of prophetic/charismatic gifts, which are evidently 'separable' from the saving functions of the Spirit described above (and neatly match what we would expect of Luke's 'Spirit of prophecy'). Furthermore, 1 Cor 12.13 can be read to suggest 'subsequence' if it may be paraphrased, 'We have all been baptized in the one Spirit for the benefit of the one body.' That is, 'We have received the same baptism in the Holy Spirit which Luke describes so that we can exercise the gifts just mentioned by Paul in 12.8–10, for the sake of the body.' (An alternative line of Pentecostal interpretation accepts that 1 Cor 12.13a probably means that by the Spirit we are plunged/baptized into the body of Christ. On this reading the reference is to conversion—but Pentecostal interpreters distinguish it from 'subsequent' 'watering with/being made to drink' of the Spirit in 12.13b.) It should be clear, then, how Pentecostals seek to synthesize Paul and Luke. Luke's view of the Spirit of prophecy fits as a smaller crater within the rim of the broader crater of Pauline pneumatology, and it maps neatly on to 1 Cor 12.8–3.

Conclusion

For Pentecostals, there is a consistent biblical doctrine of bhs. While the different NT writers expound the Spirit's roles in salvation in differing ways, Luke–Acts, John and Paul agree that bhs represents a distinct moment in the Christian life, separable from and subsequent to 'salvation.' It consists of empowering with different types of prophetic gifts for service in the building up of the church and in mission to the world. As canonical interpreters, we may harmonize the perspectives. So, for example, we may say that the Samaritans received the Johannine birth of water-and-Spirit when they believed Philip's gospel and were baptized (Acts 8.12). They received then too what Paul means by the 'Spirit of Christ' (Rom 8.9) bringing them sonship and new covenant life. But only with the apostolic laying on of hands did they receive the bhs/Spirit of prophecy to equip them for service and mission (8.17).

4
Reassessing the Classical Pentecostal Reading

In this chapter I seek to offer a sympathetic critique of the classical Pentecostal model, and point to a quite different biblical synthesis, which is still fully in harmony with broader charismatic interpretations. I will keep to the order of the discussion in chapter 3.

Assessments of the Pentecostal Interpretation of Luke-Acts

Before launching in to more specific points, it may help to highlight three major issues. First, narrative patterns are much more difficult to interpret than some readers think. The problem comes in deciding what aspects of an account Luke is commending as a repeatable (even normative) 'pattern' and what owe more to the uniqueness of the person(s) or occasion described.

Second (and related), there is a great number of 'gaps' in the texture of Luke's narrative, where the reader is tempted to fill in what is lacking with assumptions or paradigms from elsewhere. This largely explains why Pentecostals, traditional Evangelicals, and those with a more sacramental theology can all read Acts more-or-less to their own satisfaction (each finding different 'difficult passages') but still fail to convince others of their reading.

Third, there has been inadequate attention paid to the crucial questions of what Luke means by 'salvation,' and of how he considers it to be present in a community after the ascension of Jesus. By narrowing 'salvation' to little more than 'initial justification' and admittance to the people of God, Pentecostals make it easy to defend a pneumatology of 'separability and subsequence.' But if 'salvation' includes dynamic experience of the kingdom of God (as Luke Gospel suggests), how else than through the Spirit does Luke think that it could be present and maintained after Easter?

Jesus' Jordan Experience as a Paradigm for Christian Experience?

No one doubts that Luke portrays Jesus as in some ways a 'pattern' for Christian discipleship. But that does not necessarily mean he regards Jesus' Jordan experience as a simple pattern for the subsequent bhs of each individual after Pentecost. There are many aspects of Jesus' relationship to the Spirit that he regards as unique. For example there is nothing to correspond with Jesus' conception by the Spirit (1.35), nor with the 30 years of 'separability' and 'subsequence' between this and his unique messianic empowering at the Jordan. Nor does Luke think that the disciples will give the Spirit from God's right hand as Jesus does according to Acts 2.33.

Luke 3.21–22 perhaps shows that someone who is already intimately related to the Spirit may begin to experience the Spirit in a new way, empowering new tasks and abilities. But, as we shall see, this is not how Luke depicts the disciples. So we are wiser perhaps to avoid describing Jesus' Jordan experience as 'paradigmatic.' We may more cautiously speak of common elements in Jesus' experience and that of the disciples (both experience the Spirit as some version of what Judaism would call the 'Spirit of prophecy,' bringing revelation, charismatic wisdom, invasive worship, and miraculous power), while noting the differences too (Jesus does not speak in tongues; the disciples are not messiahs). It may also be appropriate to conclude that Luke considered the church as a whole to inherit important aspects of Jesus' 'anointing' with the Spirit, but it would be unwise to conclude from this that each individual believer receives an endowment just like his. For Luke, the apostles and Paul perhaps come closest to following Jesus' pattern.

The Pentecost Experience of Jesus' Own Disciples as Paradigmatic?

Here we are at first sight on much more promising ground. Between ascension and Pentecost the disciples are clearly full believers in Jesus as crucified and risen Lord, and they await the Spirit as a worshipping community with apparent prayerful eagerness. Pentecostals argue the disciples are thus surely already 'saved,' and they now anticipate the Spirit as a second blessing of prophetic empowering to act as witnesses (Luke 24.49; Acts 1.8). When Pentecost comes, Peter will promise his hearers that they too will receive Joel's promise, if they repent and call on the Lord (2.38–39), and Luke is at pains to point out that Cornelius received the same gift as the disciples at Pentecost (11.17; cf 10.47 and note the numerous parallels between the description of this event and that of Pentecost).

We need not doubt there are paradigmatic elements here. But a closer analysis once again suggests this is an oversimplification at four points.

a. Are the disciples already 'saved'? If salvation mean no more than forgiveness of sins, inclusion in the people of God, and the promise of a place in heaven/new creation, all would agree the disciples are already 'saved' before Pentecost. But for Luke, salvation means the powerful in-breaking reign of God that transforms Israel according to the great Isaianic promises (cf Lk 1.68-79; 2.28-42; 4.18-21). They taste a little of this through Jesus, and through the Spirit working with him. But when Jesus is withdrawn into heaven at the ascension there is no way for the experience of salvation to continue. Disciples can no longer encounter the person or work of the Father or of the Lord Jesus—until the Son pours out the Spirit from Father at Pentecost! So it is less than a half-truth to speak of them as already 'saved.'

b. Is the disciples' experience repeatable? It should be equally clear that no-one after the ascension can recapitulate the way the disciples experienced God through Christ before receiving the Spirit. At most they are temporarily confronted with Christ, and in a much weaker sense, through the preaching and activity of Spirit-empowered proclaimers.

c. Can Acts 1.8 be applied universally? Pentecostal interpreters use Acts 1.8 to prove that all believers receive the Spirit in order to empower them as witnesses. But this misunderstands what Luke means by 'witness.' Unlike John, he uses it only for quasi-legal testimony, that is, of an eyewitness. Only the 11 and others who have been with Jesus from the beginning of the ministry, up to the Ascension, can act as witnesses (hence the choice of Matthias from such a group to take the place of Judas, 1:21-22 cf. 10.41). Only the apostles are said to be witnesses or to bear witness. The two exceptions in Acts are Paul and Stephen. But Paul is only a witness to 'the things he has seen and heard' (on the Damascus Road, 22.15) and when Stephen is described as a witness, it is because he bears counter-testimony to the Jerusalem leaders at what was supposed to be his own trial (22.20). Others are not witnesses, and 1.8 does not directly address them. In short, in their role as empowered witnesses, the apostles are not typical. Of course, Luke anticipates that the Spirit will raise up men like Stephen, Philip, Barnabas, Silas, Priscilla and Apollos to preach the Gospel. And he no doubt expected the Spirit to inspire many more to share their Christian beliefs less formally (cf. 4.31, 8.4, 13.54). But 1.8 cannot be used to demonstrate that the essence of the gift of the Spirit is 'empowering to witness.'

d. Is Pentecost a 'second' reception of the Spirit? Unlike Jesus, the disciples (according to Luke) do not already 'have' the Spirit in any sense before they are baptized/empowered by the Spirit. That is, there is no two-stage pneumatology in Luke, with initial 'reception' of the Spirit being followed later by a second grace or second blessing of empowering. For Luke, Pentecost is their (first and only) reception of the Spirit. He has no equivalent to John 20.22. Through the rest of his narrative, the Spirit 'coming upon,' 'falling on' and being 'given to' believers is equated with their 'receiving' or being 'baptized in/with' the Spirit. We will return to this point later.

The Significance of Peter's Speech

Lukan specialists agree that Acts 2 is about Joel's gift of 'the Spirit of prophecy' promised to the whole eschatological community. But this should not be taken to mean that the gift of the Spirit is merely a prophetic empowering for mission. The 'Spirit of prophecy' (for Jews) enables all kinds of revelation and charismatic wisdom, including the sense of God's presence, his loving kindness and his guidance. So it is potentially as fundamental to the life of 'salvation' as it is for empowered service. This may explain why Luke anticipates no trace of 'subsequence' in Acts 2.38–39; the presupposition being rather that the human commitment of repentant faith, crystallized in baptism, normally receives the gift of the Spirit as the divine response. This is not (*contra* Penney) because Luke anticipates all converts will rush out to 'witness' (they do not!), but because he knows the gift is fundamental to authentic Christian life and worship too.

In Acts, the Spirit is Normally Anticipated in Conversion-Initiation

Dunn brilliantly argued that Luke (like all other NT writers) saw repentant faith, baptism, and reception of the Spirit essentially as a theological unity. There is a normal logical and even temporal order to those events, as Acts 2.38–39 implies. A person believes the good news, submits as soon as practicable to baptism (as an expression of repentance and commitment to Christ), and duly receives the Spirit as God's covenantal and empowering presence. The elements of this conversion-initiation package may abnormally get separated (for a variety of reasons), but in such cases Luke expects the situation to be rectified as soon as possible. The remaining passages in Acts more easily fit Dunn's conception than the classical Pentecostal explanations stressing the norm of subsequence. Interestingly, even leading Pentecostal Lukan specialists now agree that Luke expected the Spirit to be given without delay (for them, 'subsequence' is merely 'logical,' not necessarily 'temporal').

a. **The Samaritans of Acts 8** Pentecostals are right to assert that for Luke Spirit-reception was a matter of immediate experience. There was apparently no problem for Philip in deciding the Spirit had not yet come upon them; and when the Spirit was given it was demonstrably charismatic (hence Simon Magus' reaction). At two other points Pentecostal interpretation receives support. First (and against Dunn), it is clear that there was nothing lacking in the Samaritans' conversion—Luke describes Philips' preaching and the Samaritan response exactly as he does elsewhere. Second, here (and in 19.2) Luke evidently thinks the Spirit can be separated from baptism. But, with Dunn, against some Pentecostal teaching, it is equally clear that Luke regarded the Samaritan experience of being baptized without consequent Spirit-reception as anomalous (he would not have needed to write 8.16 if it was normal to have a significant lapse of time between Spirit-reception and baptism!). It is something immediately corrected by the apostles, without further ado. The delay is no particular problem for Luke, as he is aware that God may sovereignly withhold the Spirit until a particular occasion—as, for example, the disciples had to wait between ascension and Pentecost.

At what stage are the Samaritan's 'saved'? Pentecostals answer that the Samaritans are saved when they believe and convert. But such an answer is at best a half-truth, depending on how we define 'salvation.'

b. **Paul's Conversion-Initiation** Paul evidently came to 'believe' in some sense on the Damascus Road, and he only received the Spirit days later at the hands of Ananias. But this does not mean he 'became a Christian' in the former and received the second blessing of Spirit-baptism in the latter. Paul's 'conversion-initiation' was a more protracted process (nor was that necessarily uncommon) which was only completed when he complied with Ananias' exhortation: 'Get up, be baptized, and have your sins washed away, calling on his name' (22.16).

c. **The Conversion-Initiation of Cornelius' Household** This certainly does not involve any temporal 'subsequence,' unless one mistakenly assumes Cornelius and those of his house were already 'saved' Christian believers on the basis of 10.36–41 (an interpretation which is denied by Cornelius himself at 11.14, and by Peter at 15.7–11). But the conversion-initiation complex is held together. From their reception of the Spirit, Peter deduces they should be admitted to the church by water baptism, without circumcision. The logic is explained in 11.16–18. Here Peter interprets their experience as a manifestation of Jesus' baptizing/cleansing these Gentiles with the Holy Spirit (see below). That is, he understands their 'Pentecost' as divine demonstration that they belong—even as Gentiles—to the messianic restoration of Israel.

d. **The Ephesian Twelve** Luke calls them 'disciples' (Luke's normal term for Christians) and they 'believed' something about the messiah. Yet, strikingly, Paul leads them to Christian baptism—at this stage still a sacrament marking conversion. They were most probably then disciples of John the Baptist, awaiting the Christ he had promised. In 19.4, Paul identifies Jesus as the 'coming one' they had hoped for. Accepting this news, baptism in the name of Jesus would then be the natural way to express repentant submission to Christ. Luke does not say whether they received the Spirit within the context of their baptism (perhaps with laying on of hands following almost immediately after the water rite itself, and as part and parcel of the whole baptismal procedure) or later as an entirely separate event. But Paul's questions (19.2–3) favour the former. Paul assumes that if they did not receive the Spirit at their conversion-initiation (see their answer in 19.2!), then something was amiss with their baptism. The linking presupposition here is that conversional baptism in the name of Jesus would 'normally' be accompanied by the gift of the Spirit (*cf* 2.38–39—with 8.16 and 19.2 showing the narrator of Acts nor any other NT writer refers to people receiving 'the baptism in the Spirit.'

All NT writers most probably understood John's promise to mean that the messiah, empowered by Spirit, would effect Israel's cleansing, purging, salvific restoration. Probably none envisaged the fulfilment of his prophecy in a multitude of individual distinct 'Spirit-baptisms' (and certainly not as a 'second-blessing,' leading to the higher life!). Matthew and Mark possibly saw the whole of Jesus' activity—from his Jordan experience to the Parousia—as his baptizing his people with Spirit. They do not defer it until after Jesus' death. In that case, Pentecost would simply be viewed as a powerful event within the broader understanding. Luke's nuancing of this is relatively minor, although significant. He portrays Pentecost as the beginning of the disciples' experience of being baptized with Holy Spirit. There is no reason, however, to assume he considered it complete then. More probably he considered being baptized with Holy Spirit as a process, beginning with reception of the gift of the Spirit, but extending to include all the restorative activities of the Spirit in the lives of believers, up till the End.

If this is the case, then to transform the verbal phrase ('he will baptize you with Holy Spirit') into a noun phrase (you will each receive 'the baptism with the Holy Spirit') is potentially very misleading. The danger is compounded by the fact that, for English speakers, water 'baptism' is a discrete initiatory event, and interpreters may conclude that 'baptize in Holy Spirit' should be understood in a similar initiatory sense to denote a crisis event which leads to the realm of spiritual gifts. This, however, overlooks the fact that 'to baptize with' was quite widely used in metaphorical constructions, and did not usually connote 'initiation' (someone 'baptized with wine' was not having his first drink!).

Sufficient has been said to establish two points:

(a) the phrase 'baptize with Holy Spirit' is rare, undefined, and somewhat ambiguous; and

(b) the grammatical transformation of this promise into talk about people receiving discrete initiatory crisis-experiences of 'baptism in the Spirit' finds little basis in serious NT exegesis.

Conclusion

The Classical Pentecostal model of two-stage pneumatology cannot be found in any of the NT authors taken on their own. It can only be arrived at by a particular kind of interpretive synthesis, but one which each of the writers would find problematic for different reasons. All cohere better on the assumption of a one-stage pneumatology, with the charismatic 'Spirit of prophecy' being central to all aspects of true Christian life and service. But how does this map onto church realities today? To this we now turn.

'Spirit–Baptism' in the Church Today: Theologizing Experience

For the NT writers, then, bhs was probably a very plastic symbol encompassing all activities of the risen Lord through the Spirit, from 'new birth' and 'washing with the Spirit' to deeper sanctification through the Spirit (expressed in the 'fruit of the Spirit') and empowerings of the Spirit for acts of service (both to edify the church and to evangelize the world), all the way to the final overwhelming cleansing of God's people in resurrection effected by the Spirit. All is Jesus' 'baptizing' of the people of God with Holy Spirit. The different interpretations of Spirit-baptism today each convey an important part of a broader truth.

Evangelical and *Sacramental* interpretations point in different ways to conversion-initiation as the great transition into life in the Spirit, rightly emphasizing that it is only by reception of the Spirit that one can enter (and maintain) our communion of love with the Father and the Son, which is at the heart of salvation.

The various *Holiness movements* may have explained Spirit-baptism in a way that artificially severed it from conversion-initiation and salvation, but they have redressed the reductionist tendency to regard that moment (or process) of conversion-initiation as conveying the whole fullness of God's grace. They have highlighted the possibility of a crisis experience leading to forms of Christian life where the believer feels she is more carried along by the dynamic rush of God's grace than striving in her own strength.

Pentecostal interpretations may be seen as a particular form of this, focusing more specifically on transition to a life of charismatic expression and empowering, with the doctrine of 'separability' radically sharpening the distinction between this and the life of salvation.

Given the criticisms of the classical Pentecostal two-stage paradigm, it is not surprising there have been creative attempts (both within and outside the Pentecostal denominations) to produce a new theological synthesis that will do justice to the biblical evidence, to the church's history and tradition, and to the renewing experience of the Spirit in the churches.

Theologizing Charismatic Experience

A common starting point is a broad agreement that we do have a real set of renewing experiences of the Spirit to explain. The widespread phenomena of tongues, prophecy and healings associated with the Pentecostal/Charismatic movements, are not mere figments of religious over-optimism. It is the testimony of many that some of these gifts attended, or soon followed, a post-conversion life-changing encounter with the Spirit of God, which has introduced a new dynamic into their Christian living.

When believers with such experiences are confronted with the possibility that bhs may not be the appropriate terminology to refer to what happened to them, the usual response is to substitute other terms—such as 'filling with the Spirit,' 'release of the Spirit' or 'anointing with the Spirit'—which equally suggest encounters involving the immediate perception of the Spirit. And when faced by the difficulties of showing any of these alternative terms to be biblically appropriate, one might equally hear the slightly exasperated response: 'I don't mind what you call it, as long as you get it!'

Because of the difficulty of using any of the biblical terms above without immediately skewing the analysis, let us for the moment refer to the 'it' in question by the relatively neutral (and deliberately fuzzy) term 'charismatic-Spirit encounter' (henceforth 'ChEnc'). The question is how we relate ChEncs to the biblical understanding of bhs and to broader Christian theology. Besides the classical Pentecostal explanation, we can distinguish two other influential charismatic interpretive approaches, both of which attempt to integrate ChEncs theologically more deeply with the Spirit given in conversion-initiation.

Sacramental Explanations of 'Charismatic-Spirit Encounters'

Given our finding in chapter 4, it is not surprising that many in the Anglican and Catholic communions, have associated the gift of the Spirit primarily with baptism. This is perhaps more theologically convincing when related to conversional adult baptism than to infant baptism, but the ancient churches in the latter instance attach experience of the Spirit more to confirmation (seen as an intensification of the spiritual graces bestowed in infant baptism). If a believer were to experience a ChEnc, perhaps years afterwards, this would typically be interpreted as the 'release,' 'renewal' or 'flowering' of the Spirit given in baptism and/or confirmation.

This approach is capable of doing full justice to the fact that admission into Christian life and service is entry into that communion with the Father and the Son, through the Spirit, which begins with regeneration, and is experienced in ongoing presence, sanctifying grace and empowering. These benefits are all anticipated in the sacraments of baptism and confirmation, and a ChEnc could simply be understood as one of the more dynamic and experiential aspects of the Spirit who was already at work in believers—one perhaps leading to repeated events of being 'filled with the Spirit' for various types of charismatic service and for deeper walk with God.

Against, this, we may note two potential weaknesses of some sacramental explanations.

First, there is a tendency to spell out the ChEnc as the first conscious experience of workings of the Spirit that had previously only been inward and unconscious. An important series of Catholic consultation documents thus describes Spirit-baptism (we would prefer 'ChEnc') as that presence and power of the Holy Spirit 'given in Christian initiation, but hitherto unexperienced, [becoming] a matter of personal conscious experience.'

A weakness of this view is its failure to allow for the widespread conscious religious experiences that believers often claim before ChEncs. The view poses an unrealistic polarization between a Christian faith/discipleship, which is simply accepted by faith before the ChEnc, and a spiritual life which is also joyfully and powerfully experiential after it. While this polarity may ring true to many second generation believers brought up in the oldest denominations, it would probably be rejected by most evangelical Christians, who tend to stress a conversionist doctrine of 'new birth' followed by a deeply relational, and usually experiential, faith and discipleship.

A second and equally misleading polarization is found where ChEncs are interpreted as the overwhelming of the person by the Spirit. In this scenario, one can distinguish two levels, phases, or ways of spiritual life: (a) the 'agonistic' way, where the disciple, by the grace of the Spirit, strives to live the life of discipleship, and (b) the 'unitive' way, when, overwhelmed by God's grace, and deeply united with him, one is borne along in the Spirit, and one's life is enriched by charismata. The first way is hard work, the second is release to play. For some, this would be a powerful and helpful metaphor for the change that a crisis ChEnc brought to their lives. But to suggest such sharply divided stages represents the normal experience following ChEncs is to go not merely beyond the evidence, but against it. At best most such believers experience elements of both 'ways.'

'Non-Sacramental' Unifying Interpretations

This designates approaches for which the gift of the Spirit in conversion-initiation is given primary place, but for which the relation to baptism, as such, may not even be discussed. Under this head we may include the so-called 'Third Wave' movement (from a British perspective, effectively Vineyard Churches), as well as individual influential theologians of the Spirit, such as Thomas Smail and Henry Lederle. For the most part, these all understand bhs as in the opening paragraph of this chapter. Thus the Vineyard Statement of Faith (1994) affirms:

[We believe] that the Holy Spirit was poured out on the Church at Pentecost...baptizing believers into the body of Christ and releasing the gifts of the Spirit to them. The Spirit brings the permanent indwelling presence of God to us for spiritual worship, personal sanctification, building up the Church, gifting us for ministry, and...evangelization.

Here the Pentecost gift, which the statement goes on to affirm 'indwells every believer in Jesus Christ' as their 'abiding Helper, Teacher and Guide,' is the source of salvation (both initiating it and enabling the communion that is at the heart of it), sanctification and empowering.

This is not, however, to suggest that everything is received at conversion. Rather, believers are taught to seek gifts of the Spirit, such as prophecy and healing, and the church practises 'the laying on of hands for the empowering of the Spirit,' which, the Statement affirms, is 'often a conscious experience.' Here, clearly, we have to do with what we have called ChEncs, but they are now interpreted within a quite different theological framework from that of Classical Pentecostalism. Specifically:

1) ChEncs are not regarded as 'the gift of the Spirit,' or as the 'reception' of the Spirit, but as particular incidents of potentially many fresh comings of the (indwelling!) Spirit upon a person, performing new activities in the believer, or renewing ones previously experienced.
2) ChEncs may be referred to as a moment of 'filling with the Spirit,' but this is not understood as a fundamental transition into a relatively permanent new state of Christian existence, but as a repeatable event and/ or as the inception of some particular ministry or function.
3) There is no normative or even special association with speaking in tongues.
4) A person may have a wide variety of ChEncs—enriching their communion with God, bringing sanctifying graces, and enabling various gifts for the service of the church and its mission—but these are all rooted in the one gift of the Spirit (given at conversion-initiation), which is essentially charismatic in nature.

Essentially, this kind of integrative position works with a broader understanding of what it means to speak of the Spirit as 'charismatic.' All conscious experiences of God through the Spirit are included. No sharp division is made in this respect between moments of joyful fellowship with God, vibrant prayer, leadings of the Spirit, promptings to sacrificial giving and service, manifestations of spiritual wisdom and powerful preaching—gifts widely experienced outside the so-called 'Charismatic movements'—and the experiences of prophecy, tongues, etc (see Lederle, *Treasures*, and Turner, *Spirit*, especially chapters 10 and 20)

Pentecostal Criticisms of Unifying Accounts of the Spirit

The first is that unifying accounts dilute the distinctive experience of the Pentecostal churches. Pentecostals feel that only a second-blessing theology of the Spirit does justice to the radically new nature and dynamic of Pentecostal experience. They perceive the experience of bhs as a watershed, or, to change the metaphor, like an earthquake in Christian life, leading to an ongoing series of aftershocks. From their perspective it is inadequate to treat bhs and the initial experience of tongues as merely one in a wider series of ChEncs, characteristic of nearly all vibrant Christianity.

But we may respond that ChEncs of the type Pentecostals call bhs vary enormously in character and power. The experience is not a watershed for all, and many point to earlier experiences of God/Christ/the Spirit as more powerful. One must not downplay the new dynamic and expectation introduced, but it is partly produced by other factors (see below), and is in any case mirrored by charismatic groups that adopt integrative approaches.

The second main criticism is that unifying accounts lower the expectation of/striving for 'supernatural gifts.' Pentecostals claim that only teaching about a distinct second-blessing bhs, attended by tongues, or related manifestation, will promote biblical expectations concerning charismata. Unifying accounts cannot sustain and tradition a vibrant charismatic church.

Here we may respond that the criticism is unrealistic. Many Pentecostal churches, that formally teach second-blessing bhs, nevertheless experience very little of the charismata of 1 Cor 12.8-10, and the majority of many congregations never do so. By contrast, Third Wave congregations, who deny the classical second-blessing teaching about bhs, nevertheless often have a higher expectation of (and experience of) such gifts as tongues, prophecy and healing. The same is true of other parts of the Charismatic Movement.. Moreover, surveys suggest that expectation and experience are raised more by what the leaders themselves model, and what they teach about the desirability, function and availability of such gifts, than whether or not they embrace the classical Pentecostal understanding of bhs.

Conclusion

Pentecostalism has been a massive force for renewal in the church. It has successfully underscored the importance of 'spiritual gifts' and their role in the charismatic community. But the experience of those gifts is not tied to its distinctive second-blessing doctrine of bhs. That owes more to the history of its origins than to genuinely biblical theology.